NEW ZEALAND
Landscapes

NEW ZEALAND
Landscapes

NZ
Visitor
Publications
Ltd.
Auckland
New Zealand

The regions of New Zealand

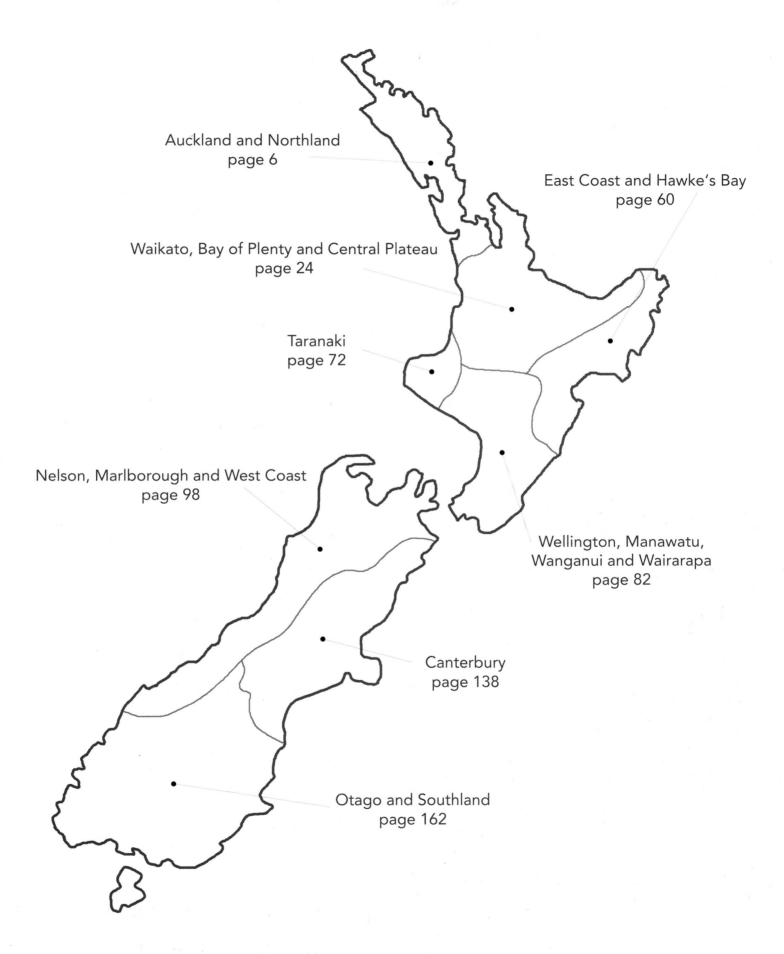

Auckland and Northland
page 6

East Coast and Hawke's Bay
page 60

Waikato, Bay of Plenty and Central Plateau
page 24

Taranaki
page 72

Nelson, Marlborough and West Coast
page 98

Wellington, Manawatu,
Wanganui and Wairarapa
page 82

Canterbury
page 138

Otago and Southland
page 162

Northland

Auckland region

The Auckland region encompasses an area of 5,290 km², stretching southwards from the northern boundary of Rodney district to the southern boundary of the Franklin district and including the islands in Hauraki Gulf. On a bed of soft sandstone formed from the sediment of a prehistoric lake, the city of Auckland occupies an isthmus that stretches 11 km between two natural harbours. Manakau Harbour to the southwest, the larger of the two harbours, spills into the Tasman Sea on the west coast, while Waitemata Harbour, the city's main commercial harbour in the east, opens into Hauraki Gulf and the Pacific Ocean.

Seismic activity caused the land to rise and erosion shaped the rounded hills and flat valleys. Later on, a period of volcanic activity on the sandstone surface gave rise to 60 volcanic cones, craters, basins, lakes and islands. According to Maori witnesses the last volcanic eruption, which created Rangitoto, took place between 500 and 700 years ago.

Hauraki Gulf Maritime Park

Hauraki Gulf Maritime Park, with its 47 islands, was set up in 1967 "to preserve this unique island and sea world for New Zealanders and for all visitors to the country". Warm currents from Australia are responsible for the unique, subtropical sea life in evidence on Poor Knights Islands. The park includes everything from islands that are just a few hundred years old to old land formations dating back millions of years.

Northland region

The region known as Northland stretches from north of Auckland to the northernmost tip of New Zealand; with its mild, subtropical climate it is one of the country's most popular vacation areas. The cleft Northland coastline was formed during the last ice age, when the sea level rose and flooded many river valleys on the mainland. This produced wide-branching estuaries on the west coast and on the east coast wide harbour basins with several islands. Further inland there is undulating hilly landscape with peaks not exceeding 800 m. The mild climate, with rainy winters and dry summers produced unique vegetation with large kauri forests, mangroves and large numbers of Pohutukawa on the coast. Northland has numerous bays, marine reserves and gorgeous sandy beaches. The giant kauri trees in Waipoua Forest and a trip over the seemingly endless Ninety Mile Beach to Cape Reinga are unique attractions form the natural world.

Double page 8/9:
Shakespeare Regional Park on Whangaparaoa Peninsula

Pages 10 and 11:
The magnificent, sandy Orewa Beach extends along the entire length of Orewa and is one of the most beautiful beaches in New Zealand. Alice Eaves Scenic Reserve is located at the northern end of the beach.

10

All pictures above:
Between and Leigh und Waipu you will find numerous dream bays, like Taupiri Bay (above right).

Below:
Whangarei Heads on the northern shore line of the Whangarei Harbour.

Page 13:
The 25 m high Whangarei Falls are probably the most photographed falls in New Zealand.

Top:
Cape Reinga rises steeply 290 metres above sea level. The Tasman Sea meets the Pacific Ocean beneath the cape. The two bodies of water crashing into one another create the Columbia Bank Maelstrom, where in stormy weather waves can reach heights of up to 10 metres. In the past the treacherous sea at Cape Reinga has been the cause of many a boat tragedy.

Above:
Cape Maria van Diemen, a few kilometres southwest of Cape Reinga.

Right:
The Bay of Islands is a large bay on the east coast of North Island and branches in many directions. The system of sunken valleys was created when several river valleys were flooded by the sea. It is bordered in the west by Purerua Peninsula and in the east by Cape Brett. Approx. 150 islands lie in the bay and the many side arms and inlets along the 800 km coastline form numerous protected natural harbours. This picture is of the historic town of Russell, one of the main centres in the Bay of Islands.

All photos this page:
Ninety Mile Beach, without doubt the best-known beach in New Zealand, is a long stretch of sand with sand hills and bush inland. Stretching along the western side of Aupouri Peninsula it extends from Ahipara Bay in the south to Scott Point in the north. Ninety Mile Beach is officially a road, though driving along it is not entirely danger-free. Numerous car wrecks testify to the danger of becoming stuck in the sand and surprised by the incoming tide, which can rise as much as 3.8 metres in six hours.

In March, having spent the summer months in the southern hemisphere on North Island and other islands in the west Pacific, the protected migratory sea birds, godwits and knots set off on their annual journey from here to Siberia and Alaska. On occasions visitors can catch a glimpse of blue penguins on the beach, or wild horses that graze on patches of grass near the water.

Aupouri Forest is growing close to the shoreline over more than two thirds of Ninety Mile Beach. 75 km long and 5 km wide it consists of imported trees, mainly pine. The area was formerly covered in large kauri forests.

Left:
Lake Ngatu at Awanui.

Left and below:
The Hokianga region stretches around the long, fiord-like Hokianga Harbour on the west coast of North Island peninsula. The natural harbour, which is approx. 30 km long, extends inwards from the coast in a north-easterly direction to Kohukohu, where it branches into the in-flowing Mangamuka and Waihou Rivers. On the riverbanks steep wooded hills protrude. Hokianga Harbour is also a system of flooded valleys, and was formerly referred to as Hokianga River. North Head (left middle) a protrusion of land at the entrance to the harbour consists of cliffs and drifting sand dunes, some of which can reach heights of 170 metres. The holiday resorts Ampere and Opononi with their beautiful white sandy beaches (below) are located on the southern coastline of Hokianga Harbour. The hinterland consists of sediment rocks and wooded elevations of submarine lava.

Pages 18 and 19:
Waipoua Forest Sanctuary is a nature reserve in the eastern part of the forest. Covering 9,105 hectares it features the last remaining giant trees from the huge Kauri forests that once covered more than one million hectares on North Island. In addition to the imposing Kauri there is also a multitude of other trees, such as liana, epiphytes, ferns and mosses. Waipoua Forest is also home to a number of rare bird species such as the nocturnal kiwi.

The Kauri belongs to the family of Araucaria plants, which belong to the Agates Australasia species, and are to be found in New Zealand and northeast Australia. This slow-growing tree is one of the largest on earth, growing to around 60 metres in height – with trunks measuring up to six metres in diameter – and can live for up to 2,000 years. Its wood is easy to process and was used by the Maori to build canoes. Commercial exploitation of the Kauri forests on a large scale first started with the arrival of the Europeans, for whom Kauri timber and gum became the main export from New Zealand. This resulted in the once enormous forests being almost entirely eradicated, with only small areas of growth remaining. Gum-diggers ransacked the earth for fossilized lumps of resin, which were used for making paint and varnish.

Far left:
At Maropiu in the Taharoa Domain there are four freshwater lakes, Kai Iwi, Taharoa, Waikere and Shag, known as the Kai Iwi lakes.

Left:
At Maungaturoto the Piroa Waterfalls cascade 20 metres into Waipu Gorge.

Below:
Farmland at Ahikiwi between Waipoua Forest and the Kai Iwi Lakes on the west coast of Northland.

All pictures above:
The wild romantic scenery of Bethells Beach frequently serves as a location for films and has always been a popular destination for Aucklanders.

Right:
Stretching for 100 kilometres, Ripiro Ocean Beach is the longest beach in New Zealand, officially marked as a road. From Baileys Beach (picture), the most common access point, you can head south to Pouto at the entrance to Kaipara Harbour and northwards to Maunganui Bluff.

Waikato, Bay of Plenty and Central Plateau

The Waikato region

Waikato describes the region around the middle and lower reaches of Waikato River, which, 425 km in length, is the longest river in New Zealand. It extends from the hills of the volcanic plateau northwest of Lake Taupo in a northerly direction between Mt Pirongia in the west and the Kaimai Ranges and the southern part of the Coromandel Ranges in the east, to a line running between the mouth of Waikato River and the Firth of Thames.

The Waikato starts out as Tongariro River on the eastern flank of Mount Ruapehu in Tongariro National Park, flows from there in a northerly direction into Lake Taupo, leaves the lake at its north-eastern corner, drops down Huka Falls and runs in a north-easterly direction to the point where it meets the Tasman Sea, south of Auckland.

The Bay of Plenty

This long, protracted bay on the northern coast of North Island runs in a wide arch from the east coast of Coromandel Peninsula eastwards to Cape Runaway, 50 km northeast of East Cape. The Bay of Plenty is considered to be the fruit basket of New Zealand, as the volcanic earth and sunny climate there produce abundant harvests for farmers.

Large pine forests have been planted in the hinterland of the Bay of Plenty, making forestry the main industry. With its wonderful golden sandy beaches, the Bay of Plenty is also one of the most popular vacation regions in the whole of New Zealand.

When Captain James Cook arrived in the Bay of Plenty in 1769, the Maori villages provided him with ample supplies of food and drinking water, which is why he chose the name.

Tongariro National Park

The landscape in the 78,651-hectare nature reserve features mountains, forest, tussock grassland and desert-like areas. The park surrounds three active volcanic peaks: Ruapehu (2,797 m), Ngauruhoe (2,291 m) and Tongariro (1,968 m). These volcanoes lie on the south-western border of a volcanic chain that extends as far as the Tonga Islands, 2,000 km to the northeast. Formed some 2 million years ago they are considered young in geological terms; they would have reached their greatest height during the last ice age, when glaciers up to 1,220 metres high extended over the slopes of Mt Ruapehu.

In 1894, Tongariro National Park was the first national park to be opened in New Zealand, and the fourth world wide. The vegetation here includes more than 500 native plants, among them more than 60 species of fern and 36 species of orchid. Up to a height of 915 metres above sea level the hardy mountain beech dominates, while scrub and tussock grasses grow up to an elevation of 1,200 metres. At an altitude of around 1,370 metres these are replaced by alpine plants, in particular the colourful mountain buttercups, which poke their heads up through the alpine gravel fields.

Rising to a height of 2,797 metres, Mt Ruapehu is North Island's highest peak. The general area of peaks, which in past geological ages was probably considerably higher, consists of a truncated cone surrounded by a jagged crowned peak. Beneath this crown, at approx. 2,550 metres and with a surface area of 17 hectares lies Crater Lake, hot, steamy sulphurous water surrounded by ice and snow.

Mt Tongariro is 1,968 metres high and the northernmost of the three volcanoes. Its peak region consists of a cone with a range of craters and crater lakes. On its northern slopes, Ketetahi Springs are located in the middle of an area of steaming pits, bubbling mud pools and hot springs and are permanently shrouded in mist from the steam of a spectacular blowhole. There are a number of still-active small caters on the north-eastern side of the mountain. The lower part of the northern side is covered in bush - mostly Totaras. Te Tatau Pounamu Wilderness Area, with its tundra-like tussock growth and sub-alpine bush is situated on the eastern flank. Rangipo Desert is a sandy, barren, windswept region in the lower, eastern area of the mountain.

Ngauruhoe rises to a height of 2,291 metres at the southern edge of North Island's volcanic plateau. It is the most continuously active volcano in New Zealand. Its almost symmetrical cone soars 300 metres above nearby Tongariro, and regularly emits steam and gas. Every few years spectacular eruptions belch ash and lava into the sky.

All photos this page
The Seabird Coast at Miranda. Countless birds, including arctic migratory birds, populate the 8,500 hectares of mud flat region that make up the bird sanctuary. The tideland's wealth of worms and crustaceans supplies the essential nutrition for the birds, which include Sandpipers, Waybills, New Zealand Dotterals, variable Oyster Catchers, Black-billed Gulls and Terns. The Godwit is one of the best-known birds in the Miranda bird reserve.

Above:
View from Coromandel Ranges of Coromandel Harbour with its many islands, the largest of which are Whanganui Island, Motutapere Island, Waimate Island and Motuoruhi Island.

Left:
Kennedy Bay is a popular destination for boat and fishing trips, especially for crayfish. In June 1867 gold was discovered and remains of the gold fields can still be seen today. The bay was named after John Kennedy, the first European settler. In 1843, after several successful years in the timber business, Kennedy wanted to sail to Auckland with his fortune of 4,000 pounds, but was robbed and murdered by the ship's crew.

Left:
Little Bay on the Pacific Coast of Coromandel Peninsula, with its beautiful beach which lends itself to all kinds of water sport.

Above:
The mangrove-lined Pitoone Stream at Matarangi.

Left:
Waiau Falls on "309 Road". On hot days the waterfall pool is a refreshing place to take a dip.

Page 29 middle:
Cook's Beach in Mercury Bay is bordered in the west by the soaring Shakespeare Cliffs, and in the west by Cook Bluff.
Captain James Cook (1728-79), the famous English seaman after whom the bay is named, anchored here on November 5, 1769 in his ship the "Endeavour". In order to determine the geographic length of the bay, on November 10 Cook and the astronomer Charles Green observed the flight of the planet Mercury through the sun's orbit. In earlier times the story went that they did this from Shakespeare Cliffs, but more recent information seems to indicate that the event more probably took place at the west end of the beach, where a memorial stone now stands. Before Cook left the bay he inscribed the name of his ship and the date on one of the trees at the water's edge, hoisted the English flag and claimed the land in the name of King George III. In doing so he "rediscovered" the country that Abel Janszoon Tasman had already sighted 127 years earlier.
This event is celebrated annually at Cook's Beach.

Above:
The magnificent 1.5 km long sandy Hahei Beach on the east coast of the Coromandel Peninsula is bordered by Pohutukawa trees and is a haven for swimming, fishing and boating. The waters off the coast form the 9 km² Cathedral Cove Marine Reserve Te Whanganui A Hei, which also includes a number of islands. Rocky reeves, complex caves and stone arches create a multifaceted undersea world.

Left:
Opito Bay is a great place for water sports and beach walks. In former times there was a larger Maori settlement in the bay, traces of which can still be seen today.

Cathedral Cove can only be reached on foot or by boat - the small bay is one of the most stunning areas of natural beauty on Coromandel Peninsula.

Double page 32/33:
View from Mt Maunganui, which lies between Tauranga Harbour (right part of the picture) and the Pacific Coast (left part of the picture) and is one of the most popular vacation spots on North Island.

All photos on this page:
A walk in Kuirau Park provides an interesting insight into the geothermal activities in the urban area of Rotorua. Visitors can observe pools with hot boiling mud, small geysers and basins with thermal water.

All photos this page and page 36:
Waimangu Volcanic Valley, the centre of another thermal region, lies 5 km northwest of Rotomahana. A walk lasting around 2 hours leads through the long valley, past geothermal attractions such as Raumoko's Throat. This is a very deep-turquoise-colored lake surrounded by scarlet red and green cliffs, which were formed when Mt Tarawera erupted on June 10, 1886.

Page 37:
Wai-o-tapu, the thermal region on the overflow of Waiotapu River, which is a smaller tributary of the Waikato River. There are a number of very interesting post-volcanic phenomena in evidence here. Lady Knox Geyser is famous for erupting every day at 10.30 am, shooting a spout of water 20 m in the air. Another attraction is Champagne Pool (page 37 bottom), a pond with hot, mineral-rich, thermal water that sparkles like champagne when you throw in a handful of sand. There are also geysers, hot water spas, mud pools, fumaroles, craters and areas where hot steam escapes from the ground.

Double page 38/39:
Whakarewarewa is located south of the city centre on the banks of Puarenga Stream and as well as being the largest thermal area in New Zealand is an important site for the preservation of Maori culture. There are numerous geothermal activities within a small area, including New Zealand's largest geyser, the famous Pohutu, which spouts water and steam 31 metres high for 5-10 minutes every hour. Shortly before, the equally impressive Prince of Wales Feathers Geyser becomes active (picture).

Above and top:
Paradise Valley and Rainbow Springs, two areas with fresh water springs, trout ponds and beautiful walkways are not far from Rotorua.

All pictures left (from top to bottom):
One of the many lakes surrounding Rotorua: Lake Tarawera, Lake Okarito and Lake Rotorua, which is famous for its black swans.

Page 41:
Whakarewarewa thermal region, which is a designated nature reserve, also contains numerous hot-water pools, mud pools and silicate terraces as well as the famous geysers.

Left:
The coast at Whakatane, with a view of Moutohora Island.

Left:
The coast at Whakatane is flanked by old Pohutukawa trees.

Below:
Huka Falls are the largest falls on Waikato River; once the river water has passed through a narrow crevice it drops 11 metres.

Above:
With a surface area of 619 km² Lake Taupo is the largest lake in New Zealand. It covers a range of indentations created by volcanic activity, is 369 metres above sea level and reaches a depth of 162 metres.

Below:
The thermal region known as Craters of the Moon, 4 km south-west of the city of Taupo. Craters, mud holes and steaming geysers form an impressive moon-like landscape.

Top:
A remarkable 15-m-long limestone arch, Mangapohue Natural Bridge traverses Mangapohue Stream. It is the remains of an underground tunnel, of which the remaining parts broke up and were washed away thousands of years ago.

Above:
Marokopa Falls are 36 metres high.

Right:
Walkway to Aranui Cave.

Left and page 47:
Thanks to its superb stalactites and stalagmites Aranui Cave is considered to be the most beautiful of the three Waikato Caves. Thousands of stalactites as thin as straws hang from the roof of Aranui Cave. The smallest of the three, it was discovered by chance in 1911 and named after Ruruku Aranui, a Maori living nearby who was hunting wild boars at the time.

Below and double page 48/49:
The best known of the three caves is Waitomo Cave. The largest attraction at Waitomo Cave is the glow-worm grotto, which is reached by way of an underground river. Innumerable luminescent insects create the illusion of an underground sky full of stars. The glow-worms (arachnocampa luminous) are not related to European glow-worms but are the larvae of a mosquito-like insect with organs in its tail segment, which produce a soft green light. These larvae can only exist in relatively humid environments and live on the roof of the cave in a kind of 'hammock' made from secretions. From there, sticky and luminescent threads hang down for the purpose of catching insects, which are then pulled up on the threads and consumed.

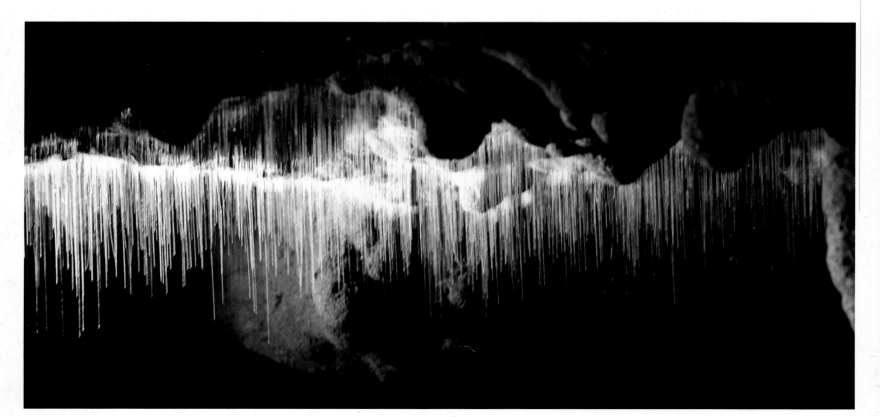

Above:
Hamurana Park, a national park on the northern banks of Lake Rotorua. One of the special attraction .n this park is the source of the Hamurama Stream. It flows into Lake Rotorua, from which more than 4.5 million litres of crystal clear water flow every hour.

Above:
McLaren Falls lie in the Wairoa River valley east of the Kaimai Ranges, 16 km southwest of Tauranga.

Above:
Okere Falls are located where the water flows out of Lake Rotorua, at the place where Kaituna River – carrying water from Lakes Rotorua and Rotoiti – spills over a narrow crevice.

Left:
Lake Whakamaru, a reservoir on the Waikato River.

Left:
Pureroa Forest Park west of Lake Taupo.

Views of Tongariro National Park (see description at beginning of chapter).

Top and above:
View of the national park from Whakapapa Village.

Right:
Mt Ruapehu, a 2,797 m high active volcano.

Double page 54/55:
Mt Tongariro rises to a height of 1,968 m high and gave its name to the national park.

Above:
Waikato River in the central part of North Island is 425 km long, making it the longest river in New Zealand. It begins as Tongariro River on the eastern flank of Mt Ruapehu in the Tongariro National Park, flows in a northerly direction from there into Lake Taupo, leaves the lake in its north-eastern corner, drops down the Huka Falls and flows in a north-easterly direction to the point where it empties into the Tasman Sea, south of Auckland.

Below and page 57:
Today Karangahake is a popular tourist destination today, with a number of attractions: vineyards, bird parks but first and foremost the Karangahake Gorge Walkway. This is a popular historical path that follows an old railway track through former gold-mining country. In Karangahake Reserve on Ohinemuri River remains of former gold mining camps are still in evidence.

Double page 58/59:
The twin waterfalls Waipunga and Waiarua in the Waipunga Falls Reserve area at the edge of State Highway 5, not far from Tarawera.

East Coast and Hawke's Bay

The Eastland region

On North Island the headland between Opotiki, East Cape, Gisborne and Wairoa is known as Eastland. Despite its sunny climate and spectacular landscape the region does not feature on the main tourist track and can be considered an insider tip. The trip along the coast offers spectacular scenery with golden sandy beaches interspersed with craggy coves bordered with bush and Pohutukawa trees. The small settlements along the route are rich in Maori culture and their artistically decorated meetinghouses are amongst the most beautiful in the country. While the East Cape coastline is a paradise for fishermen and water sports enthusiasts, inland there is hiking, hunting and rafting. Gisborne, the urban centre of the Eastland region, is situated at the heart of fertile farming country, with large fruit and wine plantations.

East Cape

The world's easternmost lighthouse stands at the summit of Opotiki Hill on East Cape. It is worth climbing the 686 steep steps to enjoy the wonderful panorama, and watching the sunrise from here is particularly special.

Hawke's Bay

Hawke's Bay generally refers to the arched area around Hawke's Bay south of the Gisborne region, inland to the Kaweka Ranges and to the main crest of the Ruahine Ranges, stretching along the east coast to Blackhead Point. The region is known for above average sunshine, glorious beaches, lush pastures, as well as vineyards and fruit plantations. Hawke's Bay wines are some of the best in New Zealand.

Te Urewera National Park

Te Urewera National Park is a 212,672-hectare nature reserve consisting of a heavily forested mountain region that is criss-crossed with rivers. It was opened in 1954 and is the third largest national park in New Zealand. The park stretches from the eastern side of the lower Rangitaiki River, over Ikawhenau Range and Huiarau Range to the south-eastern shoreline of Lake Waikaremoana, around which one of the most beautiful walks in New Zealand leads.

The vegetation in Te Urewera National Park consists of native bush, including Kahikatea, Rimu, rata and Tawa as well as tree ferns, orchids and sub-alpine plants. The tallest peak is Mt Manuoha, which is 1,403 metres high.

Top and above middle:
At Lottin Point in Waiaka Bay the quiet bays with their impressive cliffs provide excellent fishing spots. Snorkelling in the crystal clear water is also particularly recommended here.

Above:
Hicks Bay beneath Matakaoa Point, remote and beautiful.

Right:
The fern-fringed shores of the Motu River in the eastern Bay of Plenty.

All pictures on this page:
Section of coast between Te Araroa East Cape.

Above:
Hautai Beach between Horoera Point and Te Wharenanao Point on the north-western coast of Eastland

Above:
Opotiki Hill and East Cape lighthouse, which used to stand on East Island, a small island off the tip of the cape. The difficulties involved in supply boats mooring on the island resulted in a number of fatal accidents and consequently the lighthouse was eventually relocated to its present position. Like all New Zealand lighthouses it is nowadays no longer manned, but controlled by the lighthouse monitoring centre in Wellington. It is the world's easternmost lighthouse. The climb up the hill is rewarded with a magnificent view and it is especially worthwhile watching the sunrise here.

Above:
Several kilometres south of "The Three Bridges" a secondary road leads to the beautiful sandy beaches of Anaura Bay. In October 1769 Captain Cook visited Anaura Bay. A memorial plaque and an obelisk at the mouth of Hawai River mark the spot where he landed.

Above and page 66 middle and bottom:
Mahia Peninsula is triangular and hilly and extends southwards from the north-eastern end of Hawke's Bay. Vacationers visit Mahia Beach (pictured above) for its beautiful, safe beaches, as well as excellent fishing, diving and surfing. About 7 km south of Mahia Beach there is a narrow and winding secondary road to the 374-hectare Mahia Peninsula Scenic Reserve (pictured below). A loop walk leads through glorious native coastal forest containing Tawa and kohekohe trees interspersed with Nikau palms, Rimu and Rewarewa. Pictured above: Waitaniwha Bay at the entrance to Mahia Peninsula.

Below:
Tolaga Bay Wharf is 660 metres, making it the longest in New Zealand. It was built between 1926 and 1929 and enabled freight ships to land on any tide.

Left:
Mokau Falls between Aniwaniwa and Hopuruahine Landing.

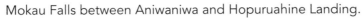
Below:
Formed about 2,200 years ago by a massive landslide that blocked a narrow gully on Waikaretaheke River, Lake Waikaremoana has a glorious location. According to Maori mythology it was formed by a water monster, a Taniwha, which was desperately searching for a way to the sea.
A "Great Walk", one of the most beautiful walks in New Zealand, leads around the lake.

Top and right:
Tukituki River.

Above middle:
Ocean Beach at Havelock North.

Above:
The area around Havelock North is world famous for its wine.

Right:
View from Te Mata peak near Hastings.

Taranaki

The Taranaki region is primarily known for Mt Egmont, which dominates the surrounding area, and for being the centre of New Zealand's dairy industry. The cows that graze on the lush green pastures around the mountain produce first-class milk, which goes into making one of the finest New Zealand cheeses.

Mt Taranaki

The symmetrical cone of Taranaki, an extinct volcano, or Mt Egmont, as it is known, rises from Cape Egmont to a height of 2,518 metres. It is the most recent of a small chain of volcanoes that stretches from Moturoa, near New Plymouth, southwards over Kaitake (683 metres) and Pouakai (1,339 metres) all the way to Mt Taranaki itself. Kaitake and Pouakai are the remains of what used to be much higher peaks that had already suffered strong erosion and were then covered with ash and stone debris from the slowly evolving Taranaki. Following a long period of inactivity the volcanoes began erupting again, which eventually led to the formation of the Taranaki cone in its present form. Its symmetry would be perfect were it not for the neighbouring cone of Fantham's Peak on the southern flank. Mt Taranaki, which, because of its majestic appearance is often compared with the Fujiyama in Japan, is the most climbed mountain in New Zealand.

Mt Taranaki's active phase ended when more and more of the volcanic material spewed from the crater fell back into the funnel, gradually clogging it up. The active energy inside the mountain was no longer strong enough either to spew out the clogged matter or to blow up the peak and directed it to the side of the mountain, where it formed the adjoining cone of Fantham's Peak. At the foot of the mountain, traces of stone that originated from one of Mt Taranaki's eruptions were discovered in some very old trees. This leads us to assume that its last eruption took place about 1620 AD.

On January 10, 1770 James Cook became the first European to view the mountain. He named it in honour of the second Earl of Egmont, John Perceval, who was First Lord of the Admiralty from 1763 to 1766. Cook described Taranaki in his logbook as "a very high mountain, similar in appearance to the Tenerife mountain."

Egmont National Park

Egmont National Park extends in a radius of 10 km around the peak of Mt Taranaki and covers 33,534 hectares. Its landscape ranges from the heavily wooded lower slopes of the mountain to the barren gravel fields, cliffs, and ice and snow regions at the peak. More than 50 rivers originate from Mt Taranaki, while chasms and river valleys with impressive waterfalls traverse the slopes beneath the snowline.

Pages 74, 75 double page 76/77:
"Forgotten World Highway" leads from Taumaranui to Stratford and pretty much lives up to its name.

Above and right:
The 2,518 m-high Mt Taranaki or Mt Egmont features a great variety of climatic zones. While there is annual rainfall of up to 6,500 mm on the western flank, the eastern side averages only 1,500 mm. This also results in completely different vegetation.
Egmont National Park, which surrounds the peak of the mountain, is one of the most popular areas for walking in New Zealand. It is also notorious for the dramatic drops in temperature, which can amount to 25° C in 30 minutes.

Left:
Paritutu Centennial Park, which was opened in memory of the first settlers, is located on the foreshore of the western city border of New Plymouth. In the middle of the park the 165m Paritutu is well worth seeing.

Below:
The coast at New Plymouth.

Page 81:
Dawson Falls in the upper reaches of the Kapuni Stream, not far from the town of Dawson Falls on the southern flank of Mt Taranaki. The town and the falls were named after Thomas Dawson, the first postmaster of Manaia and Okato, who discovered the falls in 1883.

Wellington, Manawatu, Wanganui and Wairarapa

Ruahine Forest Park

This forest landscape lies southwest of Napier. It starts with the steep gullies of Ngaruroro River and extends from there about 100 km along a mountain ridge to Manawatu Gorge. In the north the park measures up to 24 km across and in the south only 8 km or so. The Ruahine Range and its foothills lie on the main fault line of North Island. In geological terms the mountains are fairly young and are still being pushed upwards. No less than four rivers originate in the park: the Tukituki, the Ngaruroro, the Manawatu and the Rangitikei. The vegetation in the park is very varied: Red and Forest Beeches dominate the north, mixed forest and bush landscape the south of the park. The number of deer is also considerable, hence the park's popularity with hunters. Hikers and mountaineers also spend their free time here.

Rimutaka Forest Park

This small 22,000-hectare forest park is the local recreational area for the inhabitants of Hutt Valley and Wellington. It includes the majority of Rimutaka Range, which separates Hutt Valley from Wairarapa Plains. The Catchpool Valley area is particularly popular as an excursion destination.

Tararua Forest Park

This 120,000-hectare forest is situated in the direct vicinity of the urban centres of Wellington, Wairarapa, Horowhenua and Manawatu. It reaches from Manawatu Gorge in the north to Rimutaka Saddle in the south, and in 1954 was the first forest park to be opened for the purpose of protecting the ground and ground water. The Tararua Ranges are a jagged mountain range, whose highest peaks are Mitre (1,571 m) and Mt Hector (1,529). The mountain range, which forms a meteorological divide, is renowned for frequent heavy rainfall and fog.

Aorangi Forest Park

This forest park extends from Martinborough in the north to Cape Palliser in the south and encompasses the majority of the forest and bush regions of the Aorangi Mountains.

Whanganui National Park

Whanganui River is 290 km long, making it the second longest river in North Island. It meanders westward towards the Tasman Sea through steep, rugged mountain ranges. En route it is flanked by unique lowland forests, which form part of numerous nature reserves and are thus protected. Together these reserves form Whanganui National Park, which has a surface area of 74,231 hectares.

Manawatu sand dunes

These dunes have been of interest to scientists from around the world for several years. They are part of an enormous dune area, which stretches 200 km from Patea to Paekakariki and measures 18 km at its widest point. Apart from the unstable dunes directly on the coast, the Manawatu dune region consists mainly of fixed masses of sand. In earlier days these dunes were forested, but when the Europeans arrived the remaining growth was eradicated and the sand dunes exposed to the wind, leading to erosion on a massive scale. The dunes were once an important meeting point for Maori, who came here regularly to fish and collect shellfish. The empty shells that amassed at the time and the remains of the stone ovens bear witness to the course the coastline took back then. We now know that around 1800 the coast probably ran behind the first two rows of sand dunes, and about 500 years ago was 3 km further inland. Due to the strong current and westerly wind characteristic of this region the dunes at Himatangi Beach are slowly moving west. In the early part of the 19th century, Robert Wilson, a farmer in the area, introduced Marram grass in order to stabilize the dunes north of Himatangi Beach. In spite of his efforts and those of others, in some areas the dunes grew to gigantic heights, with the result that in the 1990s they began to threaten houses – a development for which initially nobody assumed responsibility. Eventually, with the help of the New Zealand army, the regional government took on the task of removing the sand from the settlements and evening it out. Since then there have been tremendous efforts to plant all kinds of grasses, trees and bushes in order to stabilize the dune landscape again.

Double page 84/85:
Typical farmland in the Mangawhero River Valley. Sheep and cattle pastures as far as the eye can see.

Above and top:
Whanganui River and Whanganui National Park.

Right:
The waters from Mangawhero River drop some 15 metres down the 50 m-wide Raukawa Falls.

Double page 88/89:
For a long time it was only possible to access the settlements on the upper reaches of the Whanganui River by steamship. The P. S. Waimarie ran from 1900 to 1949 and finally sank in 1952 at its mooring. Until volunteers began a movement to save it, the 40 years later the Waimarie lay on the bottom of the river, well preserved beneath a layer of mud. Empty oil drums and plastic containers were collected all over the city, and then attached to the Waimarie, while mud was pumped out at the same time. When the mud suddenly lost its hold, the Waimarie rose to the surface and floated. It took seven years of restoration to make it ship-shape again and it went into service again at the turn of the millennium.

Double page 90/91:
The red sandstone cliffs at Waverly Beach.

Left:
Hokio Beach, a former stop-off point for "Cobb & Co." on their way north from Wellington is located on the Tasman Coast near Levin. At the time the beach was considered the best "road connection".

Right:
Thanks to its proximity to Wellington, Paraparaumu Beach on the Kapiti Coast became a popular residential area.

Below:
Himitangi Beach is part of the giant Manawatu sand dune region that stretches northward to Patea and southward to Paekakariki.

Bays on Wellington's Miramar Peninsula

Top:
Shelly Bay

Above middle:
Worser Bay

Above:
Oriental Bay

Right:
Karaka Bay

Double page 96/97:
The Rimutaka Ranges between Featherston and Pakuratahi.

Nelson, Marlborough and West Coast

The Nelson Region

In terms of landscape the region on the northern tip and west coast of South Island is one of the most beautiful in New Zealand. There are no less than six national parks here, with exceptionally varied scenery for such a small area. The area features marvellous beaches and fiords, as well as dense rain forest with giant trees over a thousand years old, bizarre karst formations and caves, grandiose alpine scenery with glaciers which slope down almost to sea level, numerous rivers and remote lakes, swamps and wetlands and extensive native forests. Fruit and wine plantations are located in the area around Nelson and in Wairau Plains around Blenheim, where the largest vineyards in the country can be found. The Chardonnays from the Marlborough region are now world-renowned.

The West Coast

This 600 km-long strip of coastline, which extends west of the Southern Alps, emerges from an enormous area of rain forest into breathtaking coastal scenery. The region contains the largest area of protected scenery in the whole of New Zealand.

Wild beauty, strangely formed limestone cliffs, big surf and loads of driftwood characterize the windswept coastal region. Many endangered plants and animals exist in the wilderness areas along the West Coast.

The Marlborough Sounds

The Marlborough Sounds region on the north-eastern end of South Island is composed of a series of sea-flooded valleys and forested islands, and extends between Tasman Bay in the west and Cook Strait in the east. It consists of two main arms, the Pelorous and the Queen Charlotte Sound, as well as numerous other arms, bays and beaches, islands and mountains. This unique landscape was created when large landmasses sank. The Sounds were originally part of Richmond Ranges, which since the Pliocene age, 7.7 million years ago, moved approx. 53 km forward and were immersed in the sea. The reason for this land movement, which even today continues north at about 6.6 mm per year is that the Sounds are located on a line between two tectonic plates – the Pacific Plate and the Indo-Australian Plate. The foundation stone was formed some 280 million years ago. Sediment and volcanic stone, as well as a mineral belt of nickel, chrome, cobalt, molybdenum and manganese can all be found in close proximity to one another.

Abel Tasman National Park

With a surface area of just 22,530 hectares, Abel Tasman National Park the smallest of New Zealand's national parks. It is located on a promontory that separates Tasman from Golden Bay. The park's steep coastline is notable for its many bays and inlets, populated by a wide variety of maritime life including whales, seals and porpoises. The mainland rises abruptly more than 500 metres above sea level; five rivers spring from the Canaan plateau, flowing from the high plains to the sea. Inland, Mt Evand, which rises to a height of 1,128 metres, borders the park. The region is largely covered in thick native bush, including various types of tree fern and all five native beech trees as well as Hinau, Miro, Rata, Rimu and Totara. The original thick rain forest here was almost completely destroyed by the first European settlers here who cleared, burnt or deforested it for timber. On the western border of Abel Tasman National Park there are interesting limestone and marble formations. In the course of thousands of years, rainwater has washed a network of caves and tunnels into the marble stone. The deepest hole is Harwood's Hole, which extends 360 m into the core of Takaka Hill. In large areas of the park however, granite is predominant. On the coast these cliffs are battered by wind, rain and sea, all of which break down their content of feldspar, quartz and mica to expose their crystal structures. Crystals break off and mix with the sand, creating the sparkling beaches in Abel Tasman National Park.

Nelson Lakes National Park

Nelson Lakes National Park, which has a surface area of more than 100,000 hectares, extends around the two narrow glaciers Rotoiti and Rotoroa in the highlands. The two lakes after which the park is named form the source of Buller River. Mountains over 2,200 metres high, beech forests, trout streams and lakes characterize the landscape in Nelson Lakes National Park. The most significant mountain ranges in the region are the St Arnaud Range, which forms the eastern border of the park, part of Spencer Mountains in the south, and the Ella, Travers and Mahanga Ranges in the west. The vegetation in the park is chiefly composed of various types of beech, interspersed with numerous other tree species such as Kamahi, Rata, Kowhai, Matai, Miro and Rimu. Toatoa and flax can be found around Lake Rotoroa, and a large number of varied sub-alpine plants grow on the higher mountain slopes.

Kahurangi National Park

Kahurangi National Park has a surface area of 452,000 hectares, making it the second largest national park in New Zealand. It includes an area of original native wilderness that reaches from Farewell Spit in the north to Buller River in the south, and from the Arthur Ranges in the east to the west coast. Other complex mountain ranges cross through Kahurangi National Park: The Tasman Mountains in the northwest whose highest peaks, Kakapo, Mt Snowdon and Mt Cobb rise over 1,700 metres, the Wakamarama Range in the north, with Mt Stevens (1,213 m) forming its highest point, and the Arthur Range in the east, with its main peak Mt Arthur (1,795 m) and the Twins (1,809 m). The highest mountain in the national park is Mt Owen, which rises to a height of 1,875 metres.

Kahurangi National Park is notable for its great diversity with regard to animals, plants and geological formations. Ancient stone deposits dating back between 330 and 550 million years offer the best proof that the land was once joined to the primeval Gondwanaland. Enormous high plains, such as Gouland Downs and the Mt Arthur Tablelands are the oldest landforms in New Zealand, while deposits such as mica, granite and gabbro are the oldest proof of volcanic activity in the country. The numerous limestone formations are also of interest, as are the sandstone and marble caves.

In no other national park will visitors find such a great diversity of plant species; more than half of the 2,400 endemic species and more than 80 percent of all New Zealand alpine plants grow here; 67 species are to be found here and here alone. The remote landscape also offers a habitat for more than 100 native bird species.

Paparoa National Park

Paparoa National Park, which extends over an area of 30,561 hectares from the Tasman Sea to the heights of the Paparoa Ranges is New Zealand's youngest national park.

Tiropahi River, also known as Four Mile River, forms the northern border of the park, while Canoe Creek forms the southern border. While the granite and gneiss rock formations of the Paparoa Ranges are among the oldest rocks in New Zealand, the limestone rocks between the mountain range and the sea are the youngest. Over the course of the last million years the effects of washing away and other forms of erosion have created a unique landscape with deep crevices, caves and canyons, alcoves and overhangs. Rivers disappear into the earth and leave dry riverbeds and blind valleys, while the water generates extensive cave systems underground. On the coast, the rough Tasman Sea has created a spectacular coastline with unique cliffs and rock formations. Punakaiki or Pancake Rocks is probably the best-known spot on the west coast.

The lush vegetation in Paparoa National Park consists for the most part of native lowland rain forest that covers the karst region inland, an area 5-7 km across, and, given the mild temperatures, gives rise to a large variety of plant species.

Arthur's Pass National Park

Arthur's Pass National Park has a surface area of 114,500 hectares and is situated in the middle of the Southern Alps. Harper Pass in the Westland district marks its northern boundary, while the area where Waimakariri River springs in the Selwyn district forms the southern boundary. The park's exclusively alpine landscape offers a wealth of very different forms of vegetation extending from beech-covered hills in the south, tussocks in the east to the luxuriant rain forest in the west. Above the forest-line, around the snow-covered peak there are a variety alpine flowers and grasses, some of which are quite rare. At 2,270 m Mt Rolleston is the highest peak in the west of Arthur's Pass National Park. The high valleys of Mt Rolleston are covered with glaciers that spread out around the mountain. A number of large rivers such as the Waimakariri, the Otira and the Taramakau also spring in the region.

Westland National Park

Westland or Tai Poutini National Park covers 117,547 hectares from the west coast to the highest peaks of the Southern Alps in the east, where it borders Mt Cook National Park. It consists of wild coastal landscapes, lakes, rivers and lagoons, as well as dense forests and snow-capped mountains. The park's main attractions are Fox and Franz Josef glaciers. They are the only glaciers in the world whose arms extend as far as dense rain forest. The reason for this natural wonder is a fault line through the Alps created some 5 million years ago, along which deep-buried rock unfolded to form the high mountains of the Southern Alps. The geological activity along this alpine fault line has not yet come to an end, with land rising about 5-10 mm per year.

The unspoiled nature in Westland National Park can be divided into four landscape zones: The coastal zone is covered in part by stone gravel that originated in the glaciers, which in former times reached the ocean. In the second zone the ground is between 12,000 and 22,000 years old. In the flood plains farmland is predominant, while in swampy areas Manuka, Toatoa and Silver Pines grow; podocarp and broadleaf forests reign on the undulating moraines. In the third zone on the lower mountain slopes the vegetation changes according to the altitude – from dense forest with lots of ferns (up to 150 m), to forest with no ferns (up to 825 m), followed by sub-alpine bush (up to 1,220 m) through to alpine vegetation with snow grass, giant buttercups and daisies. Herbs and low growing peat grasses are characteristic of the fourth, high alpine zone at a height of around 500 m. Upwards of 2,100 m lichens that have settled on sunny rocks are the only form of vegetation. In the alpine area of the national park the mountain peaks soar to a height of more than 3,000 metres, among them the country's second highest mountain, Mt Tasman at 3,498 metres.

Above:
View of Kahurangi National Park

Middle:
Takaka foothills and Abel Tasman National Park.

Below:
Farmland at Rockville. The forests of Wakamarama Ranges in Kahurangi National Park can be seen in the background.

Above:
Waikoropupu Springs, or Pupu Springs for short, are situated 6 km northwest of Takaka. They constitute one of the largest fresh water spas in the world, with a water volume of about 2,160 million litres per day.

Left:
Road tunnel at Pohara in Golden Bay on the outskirts of Abel Tasman National Park.

Below:
View of Abel Tasman National Park.

Double page 104/105:
Totaranui Bay in Abel Tasman National Park.

Double page 106/107:
View from Takaka Hill in the Motueka fruit plantations.

Above:
South of Nelson, Mount Richmond Forest Park covers 177,109 hectares and is a popular place for hiking.

Below:
Boulder Bank near Nelson.

Above and left:
Okiwa Bay on Queen Charlotte Drive.

Left:
Governor's Bay in Queen Charlotte Sound, one of the two long arms of Marlborough Sounds.

Double page 110/111:
Typical picturesque scenery on Queen Charlotte Drive.

Double page 112/113:
View over Picton Harbour.

Top:
Hilly pastures near Lake Grasmere.

Below:
Wild calla lilies at Karamea..

Page 114 top:
View of Robertson Point from Port Underwood Road.

Page 114 bottom:
Robin Hood Bay at the end of Port Underwood.

Page 116:
West coast at Little Wanganui.

This page all pictures:
Crossing Lewis Pass at an altitude of 864 metres presents an astonishing change in landscape and it becomes quite clear how the central peaks of South Island act as a meteorological divide. Within just a few hundred metres the dry, tussock-covered highland on the east becomes dense, humid rain forest on the west. Lewis Pass lies between the northern end of the Southern Alps, which extend southwest from here and the southern end of Spenser Mountains, which extend in a north-easterly direction. During the last ice age, the mountain valleys on both sides of the saddle were covered in glaciers which have left behind steep, polished rocky crags and moraine rubble.

Double page 118/119:
In winter Craigieburn Range is a popular ski venue for Christchurch residents.

Above:
Bridge over Waimakariki River at Bealey.

Left and lower left:
Arthur's Pass National Park.

Below:
Lake Pearson is not only beautiful but also an important breeding ground for the southern crested grebe, an endangered bird species.

Top:
In an idyllic setting east of Ruatapu, Lake Mahinapua is small and relatively shallow, attracting trout fishermen, boaters, swimmers and picnickers. Visitors occasionally catch a glimpse of the crested grebe, and white heron can also be seen here.

Above:
The west coast at Tiromoana.

Right:
One of the numerous open galleries so common on the west coast.

Double page 122/123 and all pictures this page:
Pancake Rocks, one of the main west coast attractions, is located south of Punakaiki below Dolomite Point on the northern side of the mouth of Punakaiki River. These unique, layered limestone formations, which began forming some 20-30 million years ago really do look like a huge stack of pancakes. At high tide the blowholes make for a dramatic display as the water squeezes through numerous fissures and chambers in the stone to shoot up between the towering rocks in powerful jets. The entire spectacle is enhanced acoustically from the crashing and roaring of the waves reverberating in the rocky chambers.

Page 125:
Nikau palms in Paparoa National Park near Punakaiki.

Lake Mapurika, an idyllic lake surrounded by dense forest. In good weather the Franz Josef Glacier and the surrounding mountain peaks are reflected on its surface. A number of interesting bird species such as the white-throated shag, a type of cormorant, crested grebe and white heron have chosen the lake as their habitat.

Above:
Gillespie Beach is covered with black iron sand and lies about 5 km north of the mouth of Cook River. From the beach there is a magnificent view of the peaks of the Southern Alps.

Below:
View of Mt Cook.

Double page 128/129:
Franz Josef Glacier.

Double page 130/131:
Around 14,000 years ago the tongue of Fox Glacier reached all the way to Lake Matheson, 6 km northwest of Fox Glacier settlement. When the glacier receded a large piece of ice remained, isolated by a wall of moraine boulders. As it melted it turned into a lake. In clear, still weather the peaks of Mt Cook and Mt Tasman some 20 km away are reflected on the surface of Lake Matheson.

Above and page 133:
Views of Westland National Park.

Below:
One of the most popular attractions in the area is the 13-km long glacier, after which the settlement of Fox Glacier is named. Fox Glacier flows in a westerly direction at an incline of 200 m per kilometre from snow fields at a height of 2,750 metres below Glacier Peak (3,007 m) and Douglas Peak (3,085 m) at the main divide of the Southern Alps, to a height of just 245 m above sea level.

Double page 134/135:
Morning mood at Lake Paringa. The lake is situated in a low-lying area in the western foothills of the Southern Alps. It is ideal for trout and salmon fishing.

Above:
Thunder Creek Falls are 28 metres high.

Top right, underneath and below:
Blue Pools and the suspension bridge over Makaroa River in Mt Aspiring National Park.

Page 137:
Views of Hapuka Estuary Walk, a short walk through the foothills of the estuary.

Canterbury

Canterbury region

The giant Canterbury Plains consist of a long area of alluvium plains crossed by numerous rivers and river deltas. Kaikoura Ranges form the northern border while the southern limits are delineated by the Waitaki River. To the west they are bordered by the Southern Alps and to the east by the Pacific Coast. The landscape was created when sediment was washed down from the central massif of the Southern Alps and the adjoining foothills. The terrain initially drops steeply from the highland before graduating in steps, eventually reaching the coast as a flat plain. The lower-lying Canterbury Plains whose northern and southern extremes develop into grassy hills, constitute the largest flatland area in New Zealand.

Mackenzie Country

Mackenzie Country, the 5.000 km² highland region, extends west of Fairlie to the foothills of the Southern Alps. The climate in this wild, tussock-covered hilly landscape is harsh, with dry summers and cold, snowy winters.

Mt Cook National Park

Mt Cook, at 3.754 m is the highest mountain in New Zealand, is also the highest in the whole of Australasia. Its three peaks rise from an 800-metre-long crest between Hook Glacier in the west and Tasman Glacier in the east. Mt Cook towers above the neighbouring peaks by more than 300 metres and since it consists of the same stone as the surrounding mountains its height is probably due to a rapid rise in the land as the result of an alpine earthquake. On the morning of December 14, 1991 the mountain lost eleven metres in height when a mighty avalanche of snow, ice and approx. 14 million cubic metres of rock broke away from the tip of Mt Cook.

Mt Cook National Park encompasses an area of 70,011 hectares. Ice, snow, rocks, sub-alpine bush and tussock growth, as well as numerous river valleys, are characteristic of its exclusively alpine landscape. The national park extends eastwards from the crest of the Southern Alps. The 65-km long western boundary along the main divide of the Alps also forms the border of Westland National Park, while the eastern border follows the crest line of the Liebig Ranges. Almost all the Southern Alps' main attractions are situated in Mt Cook National Park: Mt Cook, after which the park is named and which rises to a height of 3.754 metres, 140 additional peaks exceeding 2,000 m in height and five large glaciers, Mueller, Hooker, Tasman, Murchinson and Godley. More than one third of Mt Cook National Park consists of areas of permanent snow and glacial ice. Tasman Glacier, which is 29 km long and up to 3 km wide, is one of the world's longest glaciers outside the polar region. The ice is up to 610 metres thick. The last occasion on which it surged forward to any degree was approx. 17,000 years ago in a southerly direction, and it led to the creation of Pukaki Valley.

Until some 150 million years ago the rock masses around Mt Cook lay beneath the ocean surface. In this period the predominant greywacke and argyle rock formations were created. In a lengthy process some 100 million years ago, the mountain chain opened up and in the course of time, as a result of erosion and the effects of glaciers achieved its present form.

The best-known example of plant life on Mt Cook is the White Mountain Buttercup, the Mt Cook Lily (Ranunculus lyalli), which blooms here in abundance. Other special plants are the snow gentian and mountain ribbonwood. The best know bird in the region is the kea (nestor notabilis), an olive green mountain parrot.

Above:
The Seaward Kaikoura Ranges run parallel to the Kaikoura Coast in the Marlborough district. They were formed some 30 million years ago by tectonic faults.

Above and page 141 top:
The rocky coast at Oaru, south of Kaikoura.

Below:
Near Kekerengu, a seal colony lies directly on State Highway 1.

Above:
On the east coast the constant wind often produces bizarre plant shapes - like here in Manukau Bay near Cheviot.

Above:
An ostrich farm near Glenmark.

Below:
Rolling countryside between Cheviot and Motunau.

Top and above middle
Woodend Beach, some 30 km north of Christchurch.

Above and right:
In Omihi Stream Valley, a tributary of Waipara River.

Double page 144/145:
Lyttelton Harbour on the northern side of the Banks Peninsula is long and narrow, part of a deep crater that formed in a volcanic eruption about half a million years ago. As a result of erosion over the course of time it grew in size.

Double page 146/147:
Banks Peninsula in Canterbury separates Canterbury Bay in the south from Pegasus Bay in the north. The headland as it is today was originally an island, separated from the mainland. Its two mountain peaks were demolished by a volcanic eruption about half a million years ago. The eruption caused two deep craters, which were enlarged over time by erosion and which now form the two harbours, Lyttelton Harbour on the north and Akaroa Harbour on the south coast. The connection between the mainland and the island was created after the alluvial plains on the Canterbury coast formed as a result of sediment that had been transported there carried there from the Southern Alps reaching the foot of the island.

Top:
New Brighton Beach is one of Christchurch's beaches.

Above:
View of Lyttelton Harbour from the Port Hills.

This page, background of double page 138/139 and double page 150/151:
Mt Cook National Park and Mt Cook, at 3,754 metres New Zealand's highest peak.

Double page 152/153:
Occupying an area of 170 km², glacial Lake Pukaki is the second largest in Canterbury. At its northern end it is fed by the Tasman River, which carries snowmelt from the valleys of Hooker, Tasman and Murchison glaciers. Stone grit from the glaciers gives the lake its milky, turquoise colour.

Left:

Lake Ohau has a surface area of approx. 60 km². It is situated at the heart of very attractive country at the lower end of the glacier valley between the southern foothills of Ben Ohau Range and Barrier Range, on the border between Mackenzie country and Waitaki district.

Right and below:
Covering some 75 km², Lake Benmore is the largest artificial lake in New Zealand. As part of a large-scale project thousands of trees have recently been planted on the surrounding slopes. The lake's water is retained by Benmore Dam and fed to Benmore Hydroelectric Power Station to produce energy.

Double pages 156/157 and 158/159:
Aerial view of Lake Wanaka and the surrounding country.

Visitors to New Zealand often come across large game reserves. In the 1960s, when the economic potential of exporting venison and antlers was discovered, wild deer were shot from planes. These were introduced species, which had been allowed to run wild for the purpose of hunting. During the 1970s, deer farming started to become popular and developed into a considerable economic sector. There are already more than 2 million deer in deer farms, most of them in Canterbury.

Top and above right:
Torless Ranges at Porters Pass.

Above:
The upper reaches of Rakaia River in Rakaia Gorge.

Below:
Castle Hill Village, a good starting point for skiing and hiking in the Craigieburn Range.

Otago and Southland

The Otago region

The area includes the southern tip of South Island and is particularly renowned for the beautiful nature there as well as its gold mining history. It is a haven for nature lovers, not only because of the unique character of the Fiordland region, which has been included in the World Natural Heritage List, but also for the higher Otago plains. Central Otago, the inland part of the Otago region, lies on an elevated plateau east of the Southern Alps. The prevailing climate can be described as continental, with four clearly different seasons, and the hottest summers and coldest winters in New Zealand. Barren hills, where tussock grass and wild thyme grow as well as numerous rivers, which in many cases have carved out deep gorges, characterize the landscape here. Though not the longest, Clutha River is New Zealand's largest river. Despite it being 16 km shorter than the Waikato, it on average carries almost twice as much water.

Southland

Southland, the most southern region of New Zealand, lies southwest of the Fiordland region and southeast of Central and South Otago and enjoys the longest days and shortest nights in the whole country. The scenery is characterized primarily by hilly grassland, which, with its lush green pastures, is remarkably different from the dry swathes of land in Otago. In this region the Southern Scenic Route, which leads along the coastline through Catlins Forest Park between Balclutha and Invercargill, is well-known for its spectacular scenery and diverse plant and animal life.

The Catlins

The Catlins region is a remote and picturesque hilly landscape at the heart of which are the 60,000 hectares of Catlins Forest Park. It is a habitat for numerous rare species of plants and animals. The list of animals that populate the waters along the coast include Yellow-eyed Penguins, Hookers Sea Lions, Hectors Dolphins, elephant seals and fur seals. The bush provides a habitat for numerous indigenous bird species. In spring the landscape is enriched with flowering plants such as bush clematis, pink tree blossom and southern rata, with its magnificent blooms.

Mt Aspiring National Park

Mt Aspiring National Park, which covers 355,518 hectares, is the third largest national park in New Zealand. It encompasses alpine mountain regions, forests and river landscapes and extends from Haast River in a southerly direction to Routeburn, at the upper end of Lake Wakatipu, where it borders on Fiordland National Park. The rugged landscape of the park was formed for the most part by the multiple changes from ice and warm periods. Mt Aspiring Massif in particular is characterized by mountains of mica slate featuring numerous glaciers, slopes and U-shaped valleys. What is referred to as the mineral belt of Red Hills in the southwest the park is a truly unique and unusual landscape – the concentration of magnesium in the ground here is so high that only a few particularly well-adapted plants are able to survive. The vegetation in Mt Aspiring National Park is dominated by Silver Beeches, which east of the divide, are interspersed with Mountain and Red Beech. In lower lying regions on the east side you find Silver Beech, Rimu, Matai, Miro and Kahikatea trees and in the more elevated regions Rata and Kamahi.

The area above the forest line is made up of alpine bush, tussock grassland and high mountain pastures, on which Mountain Buttercups, Daisies and Ourisia grow. The park is the retreat of rare indigenous birds such as the Paradise Shelduck and the Kokako. More typical bush inhabitants, such as Riflemen, Bellbirds, Yellow crowned Parakeets, Fantails and Wood Pigeons are more common. In the sub-alpine regions New Zealand Falcons and Keas are widespread.

Fiordland National Park

Extending over an area of 1.2 million hectares at the south-western tip of the country, Fiordland National Park is the largest in New Zealand. It includes the rugged coast and numerous fiords between Foveaux Strait in the south and Awarua Point, which forms the northern border, 30 km north of Milford Sound. The breathtaking scenery in this almost deserted region of wilderness is characterized by snow-covered mountains, glacial lakes, fiords, islands, numerous waterfalls, dense rain forest and elevated plains of tussock.

Fiordland's landscape is the result of an ongoing process of geological remoulding during the course of the past 500 million years. The present-day topography was decisively influenced by the last great ice age, in which the country was covered in ice for about 55,000 years. During this time the glaciers on the west of the mountains pushed towards the coast, ending up directly in the Tasman Sea. The glacial ice here was so thick that the paths gouged into the rock were hundreds of metres below sea level. When the ice began to melt the sea gradually forced its way into these paths, thereby forming the many fiords typical of this region. In the east the ice filled existing basins or dug new ones, leaving numerous lakes once the glacier receded.

The metamorphic rock forms (slate and sediment stone) in Fiordland National Park are some of the oldest in New Zealand. They were formed from lime and sandstone deposits that accumulated on the seabed some 400 million years ago. Approx. 200 million years ago, when the rocks were subjected to geological change they mixed with volcanic rock such as granite and diorite and on the surface with effusive rock such as basalt and andesite. In Fiordland National Park gneiss comes in black, grey green and white, granite is often pink and white, while diorite features white xenocryst, and andesite and basalt are mostly dark green and fine grained. The latter stone types are predominant mostly along the mountain chains in Eglinton Valley. About 50 million years ago, Fiordland was flooded by the sea for about 40 million years. Today, lime, sand, and sediment stone that are to be found in the eastern part of Fiordland between Lake Hauroko and Eglinton Valley provide evidence of this period. Some 2 million years ago the land once again rose above sea level, since when strong geological activity has repeatedly changed its form.

The remoteness of the Fiordland region makes it a popular habitat for many rare plant and animal species. Approx. 700 plants can only be found in Fiordland.

The bird life here is extremely rich in indigenous species. Dolphins, fur seals, little blue and Fiordland crested penguins all populate the waters and coast of the fiords. The fiords also feature a unique underwater world, which came about as a result of the strong rainfall in the region, adding a fresh layer of water up to 15 metres deep on top of the sea water. The fresh water is enriched with tannin washed out of surrounding vegetation, which forms a light filter for the water layers below. As a result, an extremely diverse selection of creatures is able to survive in the lower regions of the fiords, including those that would normally only be found at still greater depths.

Milford Sound and Doubtful Sound

Milford Sound is the best-known and most visited fiord on the southwest coast of South Island. The narrow sound is 15 km long and up to 300 m deep and covers a glacial basin, which was carved out of the 1,800 metre-high mountains in the area over a period of several ice ages. It is therefore not actually a sound, which is technically a flooded river valley, but rather a genuine fiord – a steep and narrow valley carved out by ice which was subsequently flooded by the sea when the glacier receded. Milford Sound is surrounded by a range of impressive mountains. The best known is the 1,692 metre high Mitre Peak, whose characteristic silhouette is reminiscent of a bishop's headgear. On the eastern shore The Lion rises to a height of 1,302 metres, and, even further in the background Mt Penbroke to 2,045 metres. Numerous impressive waterfalls cascade spectacularly down the rocky cliffs, which rise up vertically to a height of 1,200 metres on both sides of the fiord. Bowen Falls near Milford, which falls 160 metres and Stirling Falls, about half way along the eastern bank of the sound, which drops 154 metres, are the most popular. Doubtful Sound is the second largest of the 14 fiords in Fiordland National Park and has four large arms. The principal attractions in Doubtful Sound are the spectacular waterfalls such as Helena, Brown, Lady Alice and Huntleigh Falls.

Left:
At a height of 1,872 metres, Old Man Peak is not far from Lindis Pass.

Remaining pictures on these pages.:
Lindis Pass and Dunstan Mountains. The road over Lindis Pass, at a height of 534 metres, follows an old Maori route, which the Ngai Tahu used on their way to Lake Wanaka and Lake Hawea. When filming The Lord of the Rings, Peter Jackson shot the scenes in the Misty Mountains in this area.

All pictures on pages 168 and 169:
Lake Dunstan, a 26 km² reservoir, holds special appeal for water sports enthusiasts. Fishermen in particular enjoy the abundance of fish in the lake, where stream and rainbow trout in particular are frequent catches.
The lake has a marvellous setting between the Pisa Ranges and Dunstan Mountains. Making it involved flooding what used to be the town of Cromwell.

All pictures on page 170/171:

The Moeraki Boulders are remarkable grey spherical stones scattered along the shore at Moeraki. They have circumferences of up to three metres and can weigh several tons. These circular stones, or concretions, were formed on the seabed about 60 million years ago in the Tertiary Period – when lime crystals accumulated and solidified around a central core. Their chief components are calcium carbonate, quartz, clay and iron peroxide. These make up the soft stone of the cliffs beyond the beach, and with time are washed out by the ocean waves.

View from Aramoana at Heywood Point. Aramoana lies at the tip of a promontory that extends north of Otago Harbour

Tree fern at Purakanui.

Page 173:
At Purakanui Falls Purakanui River drops some 20 metres in four stages; the falls are best seen in the late morning sun.

Above, below and page 175 top:

West of Owaka, the region referred to as Catlins is an area of remote, picturesque, and hilly countryside, at the heart of which lies the 60,000-hectare Catlins Forest Park. The region is home to numerous interesting plant and animal species. Three types of penguin, including the Blue-eyed Penguin, as well as Hooker's Sea Lions, Hectors Dolphins, rare bird species such as the Parakeet and the Shining and Long Tailed Cuckoo all populate the coastline. In spring, flowering plants such as Bush Clematis, Pink Tree Blossom and Southern Rata enrich the landscape.

In pre-European times Moa hunters inhabited the bush-clad hilly landscape. Once the giant ratites became extinct, most of the Maori left the region. The first Europeans to arrive here, a group of seal-hunters, settled in 1810 at Port Molyneux, at the mouth of Clutha River. In 1840, other settlers who wanted make the most of the wealth of timber here also arrived. For a very nominal fee Captain Edward Catlin, a whale hunter, bought approx. 2,600 km² of land from the Maoris who resided there at the time. Their chief, the infamous Tuhawaiki, also referred to as Bloody Jack, was responsible for the deal. Soon afterwards, trees were felled on an extensive scale. In 1858 the first water-driven sawmill went into operation, and was followed by numerous related industries, which subsequently developed in the region. These included boat building, gunpowder production, and charcoal and leather tanning, for which beech bark was used. Initially the timber trade with Australia promised big returns, with the result that in its heyday there were 30 saw mills in operation in the Catlins region. However, once the high quality trees from accessible coastal areas had all been milled the economy in the area collapsed. Nowadays the forests are protected and timber can only be milled to a very limited extent.

Page174 bottom:
In the 1920s Cosy Nook, named by Captain George Thompson after his birthplace in Scotland, was one of the largest Maori settlements in the region. The official name is Mullet Bay.

Left:
The crescent-shaped, 19 km² Lake Monowai in Fiordland National Park was dammed in 1925 in order to provide a source for a hydroelectric power plant.

With a depth of 443 metres Lake Manapouri is not only the deepest in New Zealand, it is also considered one of the most beautiful. Located on the eastern border of Fiordland National Park at a height of 177 m above sea level, it is surrounded by rugged forested mountains. Its coastline stretches for over 160 km and it covers a total area of 140 km². The lake measures 10 km at its widest point, and 32 km at its longest. To the north Kepler Mountains rise up, their snow-covered peak forming a beautiful backdrop beyond the forest-bordered banks. More than 30 small, bush-covered islands lie scattered in Lake Manapouri, the two largest of which are Pomona and Rona.

Left:
Lake Te Anau lies at a height of 200 m above sea level in the west of Southland district, in an area formerly composed of glacial valleys. With a surface area of some 350 km² it is the largest lake in South Island and, after Lake Taupo, the second largest in New Zealand. It is 417 metres deep, 61 km long and measures 10 km at its widest point.

Left and page 177:
Images of Milford Road, which runs through Fiordland National Park.

Below and double 180/181:

Stretching for 80 km, zigzag-shaped Lake Wakatipu is the longest lake in South Island. It is surrounded by high mountains at the southern end of the central massif of the Southern Alps. With a surface area of 291 km² it is the second largest lake in South Island. It lies at a height of 310 metres above sea level, and since it drops to a depth of 399 metres the bottom of the lake is actually 89 metres below sea level. Lake Wakatipu is fed by a number of rivers: in the north Dart River and Rees River empty into it, on the west side of the northern arm Greenstone River, a little further south Von River and, at Halfway Bay on the western side of the southern arm, Lochy River. The lake flows out into Kawarau River on the northern end of the Frankton arm.

Above:
The northern end of Lake Wakatipu at Glenorchy.

Page 178 top:
The Eyre Mountains at Garston.

Right:
Shotover River – an adventure play land.

Double page 182/183:

Lake Hawea is the smallest of the three lakes in the Queenstown Lakes District and is situated east of Lake Wanaka. 35 km long and approx. 8 km wide, it covers an area of 125 km² in the trough of a former glacier, bedded between two side ridges of the Southern Alps. Lake Hawea itself is 410 metres deep and in fact reaches a depth of 64.4 metres below sea level. Hunter River, which originates on the eastern side of the Southern Alps' main divide, is the most important inflowing river. The surrounding landscape is divided into a mountainous region in the north and tussock-covered lowlands in the south. A narrow strip of land called The Neck, made from a former moraine, separates Lake Hawea from neighbouring Lake Wanaka.

Double page 184/185 and pages 186 and 187:
Milford Sound.
The breathtaking scenery of the sound can best be seen from the water. Several majestic waterfalls cascade from the cliff faces, which soar up vertically to a height of 1,200 metres on the edges of the fiord. The best known are Bowen Falls near Milford, where the water drops 160 km and collects in the valleys of the former glacier, and Stirling Falls, about half way along the eastern side of the sound, which is 154 metres high.

New Zealand – Landscapes
© December 2005, NZ Visitor Publications Ltd.
ISBN 1-877339-14-8

Editing, layout and typesetting:
NZ Visitor Publications Ltd., 188 Quay Street, Auckland, New Zealand
Photographs:
Helga Neubauer, NZ Visitor Publications Ltd., 188 Quay Street, Auckland, New Zealand.
Supplied by Werner Weiler: Page 10 left above and left middle. Page 11 whole page,
page 12 left, 3 top pictures and above right, page 15 whole page, page 23 whole page,
page 24 and 25 background picture, page 26 whole page, page 28 left below, page 30
and 31 all pictures, page 32 and 33, page 34 all pictures, page 45, page 46 and 47 all
pictures, page 48 and 49, page 74 left below, page 75 and 76, page 110 and 111, page
124 all pictures, page 136 and 137 all pictures, page 146 and 147, page 148 left above,
page 150 and 151, page 152 and 153, page 156 and 157, page 158 and 159, page 160 all
pictures, page 179 left below, page 182 and 183, page 184 and 185, page 186 and 187
all pictures, page 188 and 189.
Maps:
NZ Visitor Publications Ltd., 188 Quay Street, Auckland, New Zealand
Editorial office:
NZ Visitor Publications Ltd., 188 Quay Street, Auckland, New Zealand
Printing:
Alpina Druck, Innsbruck, Austria

The publisher cannot accept responsibility for the contents in this book.
We cannot guarantee that this book has not been struck by erronitis. Should this be the
case, we would be grateful if you could point out any errors to us. Please write to:
NZ Visitor Publications Ltd.
188 Quay Street, Auckland, New Zealand
or via e-mail:
editor@nzpublications.com